Zoom in on
CAREGIVING ROBOTS

Jill Sherman

Enslow Publishing
101 W. 23rd Street
Suite 240
New York, NY 10011
USA
enslow.com

WORDS TO KNOW

artificial intelligence Software that allows a computer to reason and learn.

computer A programmable machine.

invent To make something new.

machine A device that people operate.

program A set of computer instructions.

robot A programmable machine that can carry out a series of actions by itself.

sensor A part of a robot that helps it understand the world around it. Sensors detect light, temperature, pressure, sound, or motion.

CONTENTS

This robot can help this woman walk.

Bots That Care

Grandma has her very own robot! It helps her every day. Grandma takes a lot of medicine. She takes different pills at different times. When she wakes up, the robot gives her a pill.

Grandma also has a hard time moving around. The robot helps her out of bed. It stays with her. She gets dressed. She takes a shower. The robot is never far away.

Robot pets can keep people company in their homes. The robot has sensors to detect the things around it.

Later, the robot gives her a checkup. It takes her temperature. It listens to her heart. It measures her blood pressure. Then it calls her doctor. The doctor looks at the robot's work. He asks how Grandma is feeling. The doctor changes her medicine and updates the robot. Talk about a house call!

Robot Numbers

There are more than eight million robots in use around the world today.

Help at Home

Some people need 24-hour care. But family members can't always be there. And home health care is expensive. Why not give the task to robots?

We already use machines to do many daily tasks. So how are robots any different? A robot is still a machine. But robots "know" what they are doing. You do not need to operate a robot. Set the robot to work. Then walk away. The robot does not need your help. It already knows its task.

Plus, robots can sense the world around them. You have five senses. They are sight, sound, smell, taste, and touch. Robots need senses, too. That is why they have sensors.

Robot Design

Robots can help in many ways. But making a robot that works takes time. Many parts have to work together. And it has to work without you.

Robot Bodies

First comes the body. Robots come in all shapes and sizes. It just depends on what their job will be. For example, a robot that helps people move around would need a large body.

A vacuum robot is built small and low. It will run along the floor to pick up dirt.

It needs to support a person's weight. But a robot that helps to clean the floor can be smaller. Its body does not need to reach high off the ground.

A robot also needs moving parts. But not all robots move from one place to another. If so, it may just have a moveable arm or grippers. Such a robot could prepare daily medicine. It stays in one spot. Its arms select the right pills.

Brain Power

A robot needs to know what to do. It needs a computer. The computer is the robot's "brain." The computer has the robot's instructions. The instructions are a program.

Special Parts

Robots that go need special parts. Many use wheels. But if the robot will be moving outside it may have tracks, as on a tank.

If the robot has to climb stairs, it may have legs!

Sensors let the robot sense the world. What sensors it uses depends on the job. If it operates by voice command, it will need a microphone to hear you. If it has to pick something up, then it will need a camera to spot the object. A robot that fetches objects needs a camera.

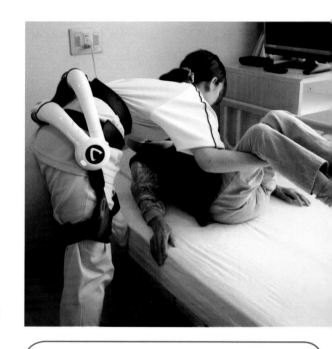

A robotic helper fits onto a nurse's body. It helps move her when she lifts a patient.

12

Helping Hands

Being sick can be lonely. It is hard to get around. Some people rarely leave their homes. That is why scientists made PARO.

PARO is a companion robot. It looks like a baby seal. PARO moves like it is alive. The bot moves its head, blinks, and squeaks. When you stroke it, PARO remembers what actions it did. Then it does them again.

The robot helps patients with stress. They feel calm when they pet the fuzzy bot. PARO can sense touch. It can see light

A robot that looks like a baby seal can help people who are lonely. Touch its fur and watch it move.

and dark. It can even hear you when you say its name.

Nursing Care

Some people need constant medical care. They may have a nurse come to help. But this can be expensive. Robots can help with a nurse's job. They give you medicine. They take your temperature. They check your pulse. They talk to you about your health. And they tell important information to your doctor.

Robots can also draw blood. Put your arm in place. The robot uses special cameras to spot your veins. Then it aligns the needle. In under a minute you are done. The bot does the job just as well as trained staff.

Helping Hands

People who are sick or injured or have a disability may need extra help. Robots allow them to help themselves. Some people have trouble moving around. A little extra help can go a long way. Robots can come to the rescue.

Tiny Bots

The smallest robots are called nanobots. You would need a microscope to see them. Doctors use nanobots to treat injuries and illnesses.

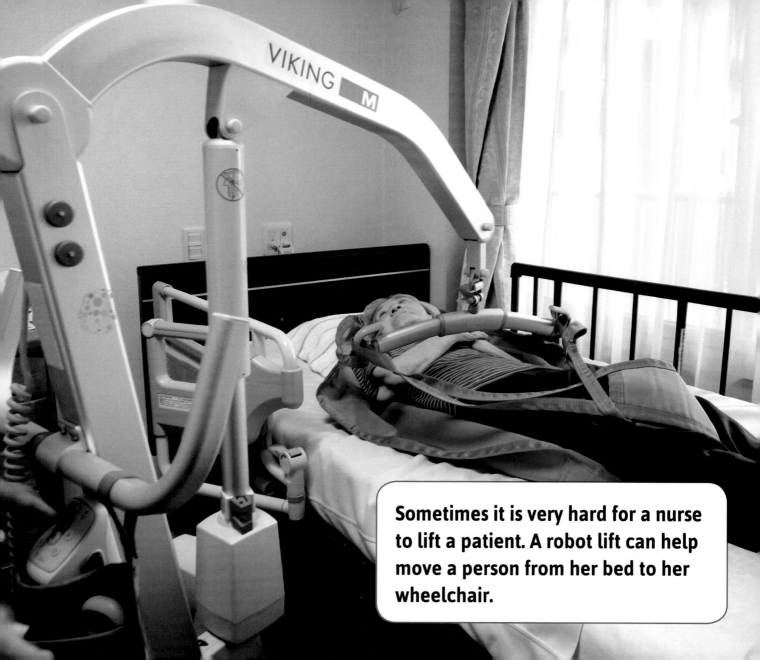

Sometimes it is very hard for a nurse to lift a patient. A robot lift can help move a person from her bed to her wheelchair.

Now you're settled on the sofa. But your glasses are on the other side of the room! With an El-E fetching bot, you can sit pretty. Identify the item you need with a laser pointer. The bot will roll to where you pointed. El-E lowers its arm. Its gripper picks up the glasses. It saved you a lot of trouble.

Cleaning robots help with chores. One robot can vacuum the rugs. One can mop the floor. Another can mow the lawn. With robot help, people can live happy and healthy lives.

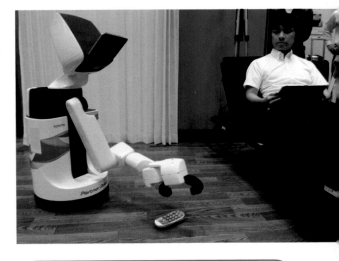

Don't worry if you can't reach the remote control! This robot will pick it up and bring it to you.

Our Robotic Future

Imagine a future full of robots. Not feeling well? Just call your home's robot doctor. Need to go to the hospital? It would be staffed with robots. Doctors could care for patients. The robots could run tests and deliver medicine.

Giving Out Medicine

In some places, robot pharmacies are already helping. Patients all have special medications. Someone has to get the pills.

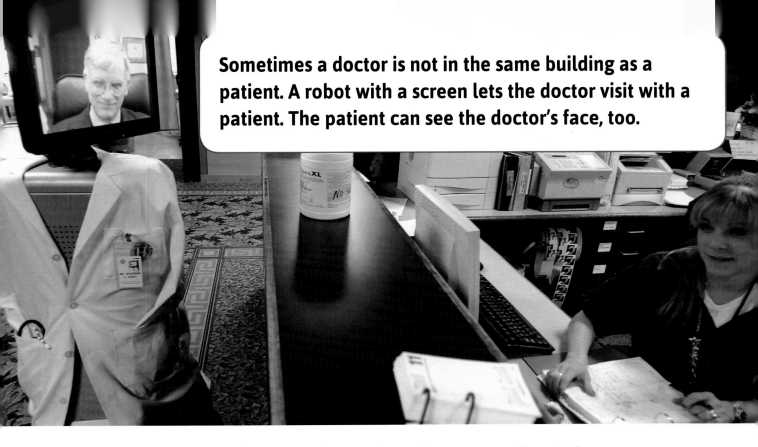

Sometimes a doctor is not in the same building as a patient. A robot with a screen lets the doctor visit with a patient. The patient can see the doctor's face, too.

They have to check the dose. Then they count the right number. They put the pills in labeled packages. Robots can do this all much faster than a person. And they are error-free!

Now put those pills on a Tug robot and let it deliver pills around the hospital!

Smart Robots

Every day, scientists are inventing and improving robots. Robots are getting smarter all the time. One of the biggest improvements is in artificial intelligence, or AI. AI is software for the robot. It helps the robot reason and learn. AI tries to think like a human.

For example, some robots take voice commands. But you may have to say specific words. You say, "Robot, pick

Smarts

Watson is a robot with artificial intelligence. Scientists from IBM designed it to play *Jeopardy!* In 2011, Watson defeated the top human champions on the show.

up my book on the table."
With better AI, you can talk
to your robot like another
person. You could say, "Hey
Robot, grab my book from
the kitchen" or "Can you find
my book, Robot?"

With new improvements,
robots can help care for
people in new ways. The
future of caregiving robots
looks bright.

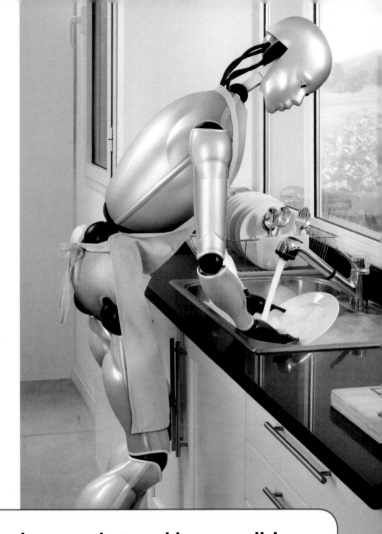

Some day in the future, you may have a robot washing your dishes. As artificial intelligence, or AI, develops, robots will keep getting more and more helpful.

ACTIVITY:
PROGRAM YOUR FRIEND

Robots must follow their programs. They only perform the instructions. Nothing more. Can you give instructions like a programmer?

What you'll need:

paper

pencil

friend

1. Pick a task you want your friend to do. Make it simple. You could have them fill a glass of water.

2. Write down detailed instructions. Think through the whole process. For example: "Open the cabinet. Move your hand to the bottom shelf. Grip the glass."

3. When you're done. Read your instructions aloud. Your friend should do EXACTLY what you have written. Nothing more.

4. Was your program a success? Or did you forget something? Maybe you left the water running in the sink. This is a "bug" in the program.

5. Debug your program. Rewrite the instructions until it is successful.

LEARN MORE

Books

Stewart, Melissa. *National Geographic Readers: Robots.* New York, NY: National Geographic Children's Books. 2014.

Tuchman, Gail. *Robots.* New York, NY: Scholastic, 2015.

Zuchora-Walske, Christine. *Robots at Home.* Minneapolis, MN: Lerner Books. 2014.

Websites

Galileo Educational Network: Robotics
galileo.org/robotics
This site engages students in science and engineering by giving them the tools to invent and build using digital technology.

Idaho Public Television Dialogue for Kids: Robots
idahoptv.org/sciencetrek/topics/robots
Watch helpful videos showing how robots are used everywhere from work to home.

INDEX

Published in 2018 by Enslow Publishing, LLC.
101 W. 23rd Street, Suite 240, New York, NY 10011

Printed in the United States of America

Library of Congress Cataloging-in-Publication Data

Names: Sherman, Jill., author.
Title: Zoom in on caregiving robots / Jill Sherman.
Description: New York : Enslow Publishing, 2018. | Series: Zoom in on robots | Includes bibliographical references and index.
Identifiers: LCCN 2017021489| ISBN 9780766092297 (library bound) | ISBN 9780766094406 (pbk.) | ISBN 9780766094413 (6 pack)
Subjects: LCSH: Robots—Juvenile literature. | Robotics—Juvenile literature. | Artificial intelligence—Juvenile literature.
Classification: LCC TJ211.2 .S5385 2018 | DDC 629.8/93—dc23
LC record available at https://lccn.loc.gov/2017021489